ASTROLOGICA

written by
Suki Ferguson

illustrated by
Camelia Pham

WIDE EYED EDITIONS

CONTENTS

- 4 ◆ Introduction
- 6 ◆ Glossary

8 ◆ THE ORIGINS OF ASTROLOGY

- 10 ◆ Map, Clock and Calendar

12 ◆ MYTHS OF THE TROPICAL ZODIAC

- 14 ◆ Aries
- 16 ◆ Taurus
- 18 ◆ Gemini
- 20 ◆ Cancer
- 22 ◆ Leo
- 24 ◆ Virgo
- 26 ◆ Libra
- 28 ◆ Scorpio
- 30 ◆ Sagittarius
- 32 ◆ Capricorn
- 34 ◆ Aquarius
- 36 ◆ Pisces

38 ◆ MYTHS OF THE SOLAR SYSTEM

- 40 ◆ The Sun
- 42 ◆ Mercury
- 44 ◆ Venus
- 46 ◆ Earth
- 48 ◆ The Moon
- 50 ◆ Mars
- 52 ◆ Jupiter
- 54 ◆ Saturn
- 56 ◆ Uranus
- 58 ◆ Neptune
- 60 ◆ Pluto

62 ◆ MYTHS OF THE STARS

- 64 ◆ The Milky Way
- 66 ◆ Sirius
- 68 ◆ Ursa Major
- 70 ◆ Yacana
- 72 ◆ Hikoboshi and Orihime
- 74 ◆ Māui's Fish Hook
- 76 ◆ Cassiopeia
- 78 ◆ The Wayfinder's Friend
- 80 ◆ Orion's Belt
- 82 ◆ The Four Stags
- 84 ◆ The Seven Star-Sisters

86 ◆ **STAR KNOWLEDGE AROUND THE WORLD**

88 ◆ A Compass Made of Stars

90 ◆ The City Calendars of the Maya

92 ◆ The Children of the Sun

94 ◆ Aztec Sun Sacrifices

96 ◆ Emperors, Asterisms and Eclipses

98 ◆ The Chinese Zodiac

100 ◆ The Great Race

102 ◆ **ASTROLOGY TODAY**

104 ◆ Astrology and Astronomy

106 ◆ A Key to Understanding

108 ◆ **DEAR STAR-SEEKER**

110 ◆ Index

INTRODUCTION

Welcome, dear reader, to a multiverse of stars, animals, symbols and stories.

Across all remembered time, people have woven tales that connect us to the most distant objects in our universe — the whirling orbs of rock and gas that make up the planets in our solar system, and the stars that sparkle in the dark, existing as suns in universes beyond our own.

Astrologica is your guide to the seeds of astronomy, looking back thousands of years to a time when storytellers in every culture looked to the skies. Using observation and imagination, astrologers created powerful myths to help others remember the maps above our heads.

There are many astrological tales to be told. Exploring the zodiac world introduces us to the antics of gods and monsters, and celebrations of animal and plant magic. Today, some of these ancient zodiacs are rarely spoken of, while others come up in day-to-day conversation all the time.

Through these star stories, we can travel from the Earth to the heavens and back again — and our journey begins here. . .

GLOSSARY

Asterism — a cluster of stars that form a distinctive pattern. Some asterisms sit within a larger constellation, and others exist in their own bit of space.

Astrology — the belief that the movements of stars and planets influence our lives here on planet Earth. This could be either symbolically or directly.

Astronomy — the study of all matter beyond our atmosphere. Where the skies of Earth end, astronomy begins. An astronomer may study the composition of stars, planets and tiny particles of space dust; the structure of faraway galaxies; and the laws of physics in space.

Constellation — a large group of stars that form a pattern that is so well known that they have been given a particular name. There are eighty-eight officially recognised constellations, and each one has a distinctive appearance.

Cosmos — everything that exists beyond (and including) our galaxy. We sit within the unimaginable vastness of the cosmos. In the cosmos, many galaxies are held together in a natural system. 'The universe' is another way of referring to the cosmos.

Folklore — stories and customs that make one culture different from another. Myths are part of folklore, but a folktale need not be a myth; they are often funny or scary stories about local animals, spirits and ordinary people.

Galaxy — a galaxy is a specific force field within the universe. Everything within one (planets, stars, dust and gas) is held by gravity. There are probably more than 200 billion different galaxies, and a large galaxy can contain other smaller ones.

Mesopotamia — an ancient region in modern-day Iraq.

(The) Milky Way — a hazy band of starlight in our night sky: the vast spiral galaxy that contains our own (much smaller) group of planets – the Solar System.

Millennia — the plural of millennium. It is a term often used to describe a period of undetermined length.

Myth — a legend that has been told for many years and suggests how the world came to be the way it is. Different cultures have their own myths. Facts don't matter in myths; instead, myths tend to be about gods, right and wrong, and how to live in harmony with nature.

Solar System — the name of our planetary system. The word 'solar' relates to our Sun, and the 'system' around it includes eight planets (including Earth) and hundreds of moons.

Zodiac — a zodiac is a system used by astrologers to map the position of the stars in the night sky. When the Sun aligns with a particular group of stars — a constellation — these stars are referred to as a zodiac symbol or star sign.

THE ORIGINS OF ASTROLOGY

The skies above us are ever-changing yet eternal. No one knows when we humans first truly noticed the sky — it was so many tens of thousands of years ago. And yet our awareness of Earth's place in the cosmos is something that makes us different from other living things.

Over millennia, people have looked to the Sun, Moon and stars in the same way we look at maps and clocks today. And all through history, in every part of the world, we have told each other stories of the stars. . .

MAP, CLOCK AND CALENDAR

Imagine this: you live in an era where the Sun, Moon and stars are a constant topic of conversation. Across the Americas, Oceania, Africa, Europe and Asia, the stars are clear at night — no electricity clouds the dark.

Wherever you are, you and your family pay attention to the sky above, for it tells you which direction to travel in, when days will grow longer and when the season will change. The sky is your map, your clock and your calendar...

◇ **Around 65,000 years ago...**
By following the stars, seafaring people navigate boats to the land we now call Australia. The plants, animals and constellations become their guides.

◇ **More than 5,000 years ago...**
People make the Pacific Islands home by sailing across the biggest ocean on the planet. Islanders interpret the stars, enabling them to travel thousands of kilometres without maps or compasses.

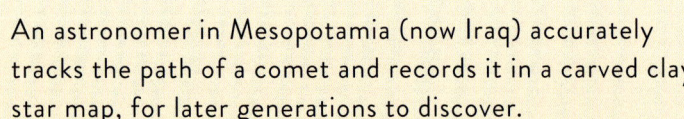

An astronomer in Mesopotamia (now Iraq) accurately tracks the path of a comet and records it in a carved clay star map, for later generations to discover.

In ancient Ethiopia, observation of the Moon and her cycles inspire the creation of a calendar of thirteen months rather than twelve. There are thirty days in twelve of the months and five days in the thirteenth. This calendar is still used in Ethiopia today.

◇ **Between 3,000 and 500 years ago...**
In ancient Central America, the Maya carve the paths of celestial objects into the walls of their temples, and later, the Aztecs worship the Sun so fervently they offer it human sacrifices. Both empires plan ritual days using solar calendars made of overlapping circles.

In ancient South America, the Inca people build sacred observatories high in the Andean mountains so that the stars can be interpreted by priest-astronomers.

◇ **Around 1,200 years ago...**
In China, astronomers map out more than 1,300 stars in special catalogues. The movement of stars is recorded nightly and used to advise emperors on how best to govern.

◇ **And around 500 years ago...**
In India, astronomers build gigantic, yet precise, instruments that measure the orbits of the planets with great accuracy.

In Italy, a physicist uses magnifying lenses to study the planets and proves that Earth revolves around the Sun, rather than the other way around.

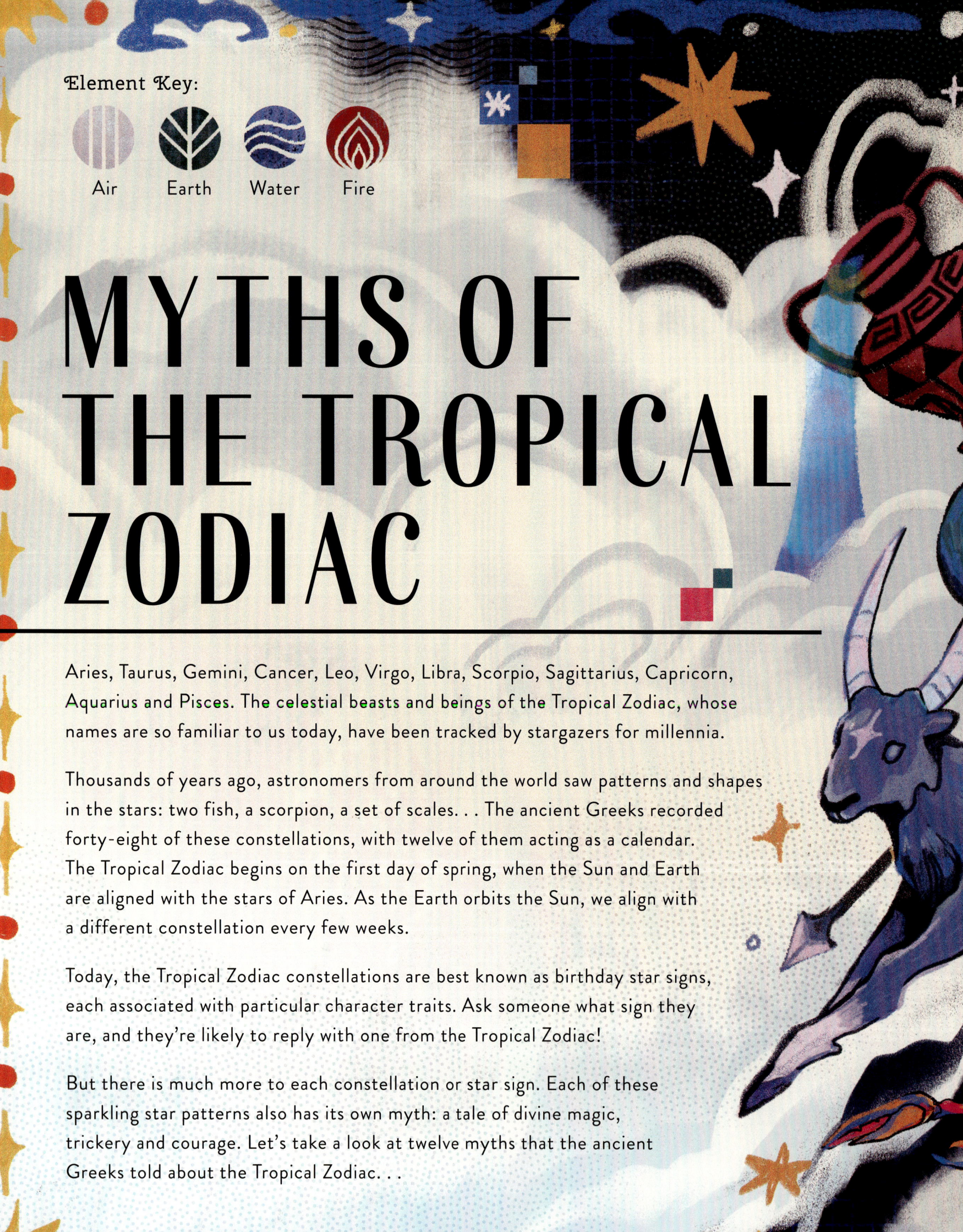

Element Key:

Air   Earth   Water   Fire

MYTHS OF THE TROPICAL ZODIAC

Aries, Taurus, Gemini, Cancer, Leo, Virgo, Libra, Scorpio, Sagittarius, Capricorn, Aquarius and Pisces. The celestial beasts and beings of the Tropical Zodiac, whose names are so familiar to us today, have been tracked by stargazers for millennia.

Thousands of years ago, astronomers from around the world saw patterns and shapes in the stars: two fish, a scorpion, a set of scales. . . The ancient Greeks recorded forty-eight of these constellations, with twelve of them acting as a calendar. The Tropical Zodiac begins on the first day of spring, when the Sun and Earth are aligned with the stars of Aries. As the Earth orbits the Sun, we align with a different constellation every few weeks.

Today, the Tropical Zodiac constellations are best known as birthday star signs, each associated with particular character traits. Ask someone what sign they are, and they're likely to reply with one from the Tropical Zodiac!

But there is much more to each constellation or star sign. Each of these sparkling star patterns also has its own myth: a tale of divine magic, trickery and courage. Let's take a look at twelve myths that the ancient Greeks told about the Tropical Zodiac. . .

ARIES

SEASON: Around 21st March until around 19th April

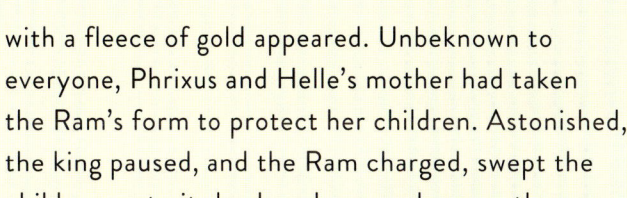

◇ **Aries Star Sign Traits:**
- Strong-willed with lots of enthusiasm.
- Courageous and enjoys adventure.
- Loves to compete (and win!).
- Impatient at times.

Constellation   Symbol   Element

The Ram appears in the myth of Phrixus and Helle, who were children of a Theban king. When the king took a new queen, the children's mother left the kingdom, cursing the crops as she went. The king sent his messenger to the oracle to ask how he might prevent his people from starving. However, the new queen hated Helle and Phrixus, and she bribed the king's messenger to lie about them. The messenger told the king that the oracle said: 'For the crops to grow once more, you must sacrifice your children.'

The king agreed to make the sacrifice. Phrixus and Helle were brought before him — but as the king prepared to strike his son, a dazzling winged Ram with a fleece of gold appeared. Unbeknown to everyone, Phrixus and Helle's mother had taken the Ram's form to protect her children. Astonished, the king paused, and the Ram charged, swept the children on to its back and escaped across the sea.

The flight across the sea took a long time, and Helle grew very cold and tired. She tried to hang on to the Ram's golden wool and stay warm, but eventually her strength gave out, and she slipped and fell into the waves below. She drowned, and only Phrixus arrived safely.

Not knowing that the Ram was his mother, Phrixus believed that it had been sent by the gods. He was grateful and wanted to say thank you to the gods for their protection, and so he sacrificed his rescuer.

The Ram became the constellation we call Aries. Its mythic golden fleece was placed in a temple in a sacred forest, where it was guarded by a dragon who never slept.

TAURUS

SEASON: Around 20th April until around 20th May

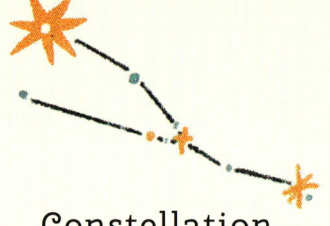  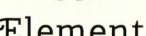

Constellation   Symbol   Element

The stars that make up Taurus in the night sky have been known to stargazers since the Bronze Age, many years before the ancient Greeks came to give it its famous name. The Bull of this zodiac myth is as strong as you would imagine — and a little bit deceptive, too.

Picture a magnificent white beast, with curving, cream-coloured horns, long eyelashes and a pink nose, standing peacefully in a flowery meadow. The warm sun makes the bull drowsy and sweet-natured, easy to approach and greet with a pat on its warm, rounded flank.

This is Taurus, the Bull that the beautiful nymph Europa met one day. She was a divine spirit of the rivers who often walked through this valley of wildflowers. Charmed by the Bull's gentle presence, she had no idea that it was really Zeus, the god of all gods, and that he was playing a trick on her.

When the Bull knelt before Europa, she climbed atop his broad back. As soon as she did, the Bull stole her away, galloping all the way to the island of Crete. There, he became Zeus and gave Europa all the gifts she could dream of.

Europa grew to love Zeus, and they had three sons. The last of these became King Minos, who kept the Minotaur, a creature half-man, half-bull, in a labyrinth. King Minos led a cult of bull worship, where followers gave tribute to Zeus through the form of these magnificent and unpredictable beasts.

Zeus himself was fond of bulls, and he named the bull constellation Taurus so that he would always be associated with this animal in the stars.

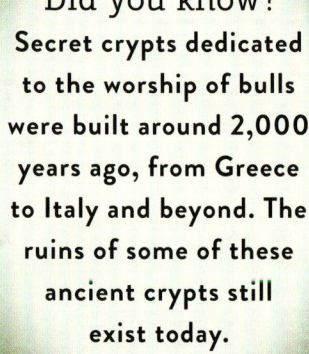

Did you know?
Secret crypts dedicated to the worship of bulls were built around 2,000 years ago, from Greece to Italy and beyond. The ruins of some of these ancient crypts still exist today.

◇ **Taurus Star Sign Traits:**
- Calm, practical and reliable.
- Affectionate and prefers comfort to adventure.
- Stubborn — unlikely to give way or compromise.

GEMINI

SEASON: Around 21st May until around 21st June

◇ **Gemini Star Sign Traits:**
- Entertaining, quick-witted and expressive.
- Loves meeting new people and exploring new places.
- Curious and scatty — involved in everything!

The story of the Gemini constellation centres around the unwavering love between twin brothers. These twins began life in unusual circumstances: they were not born — they hatched, fully formed, from a giant egg instead. They were identical in almost every way: although they shared a mother — Leda, the Spartan queen — the twin boys did not share a father. One twin, Pollux, was a son of Zeus. The other twin, Castor, was son to a Spartan king. Neither twin knew that Pollux was immortal, unlike Castor, who was fated to die.

Pollux and Castor grew up together and became renowned as talented boxers and unmatched horsemen. People travelled great distances to present them with fine horses, whom they trained for chariot racing, boar-hunting and battle.

Pollux and Castor had enemies, however. They married two sisters from a family of rival horsemen, but did not seek proper permission. The sons from this family stole their prized horses and cattle in revenge. The twins went to free their stolen animals in the dead of night, but the rival's sons had stayed up late to keep watch. They caught Castor and stabbed him with a spear. The rivals went to kill Pollux, but Zeus protected his son by raining thunderbolts down on his attackers.

Pollux was distraught when he realised that his beloved brother was dying. Zeus felt sorry for his son and gave him a choice: he could share his immortality with Castor — but they could never be together again. Pollux accepted, and the brothers took turns between dwelling in the underworld and dwelling in the heavens. They live on forever as the two brightest stars in the constellation of Gemini, on either side of the equatorial line that divides the night skies.

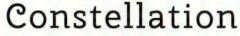
Constellation

Symbol

Element

Did you know?
In ancient Arabian astrology, these twin stars were thought to embody a pair of proud, beautiful peacocks — just like mythic descriptions of Queen Leda's proud, beautiful sons.

CANCER

◇ **Cancer Star Sign Traits:**
- A sensitive soul who feels things deeply.
- Enjoys being at home and is fond of little comforts.
- Can be guarded, but is devoted to the people they trust.

SEASON: Around 22nd June until around 22nd July

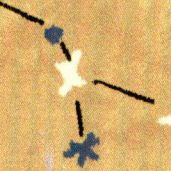  

Constellation   Symbol   Element

The Great Crab lived for centuries in the marshes of a dark lake. She had a wide, strong shell, the colour of wet stone. Her eight legs ended in delicate points, allowing her to scuttle lightly across the silent lake bed. The marshes were her home, and she was beloved by the goddess Hera.

The Great Crab paid little attention to the world above, until one day she heard the heavy thuds of footsteps, then splashes. Next, she saw huge legs, like the trunks of trees, stirring up the fine silt. Looking up, the surface glimmered, obscuring her vision of a giant's body swaying above. She heard muffled roars, and then she saw the snaking, many-headed body of the Hydra, thrashing in the depths.

The Hydra had helped the Great Crab when heat had burnt away the marsh waters. The Sun had seared the Great Crab's shell, and she'd sought refuge in the damp cave where the Hydra lived. The air stank of the Hydra's venomous breath, and the Hydra's many snake-heads hissed at the Great Crab at first, but then they grew accustomed to each other. Together, they had waited for the rains to return.

Seeing the Hydra under attack angered the Great Crab, and she moved to defend her friend. With sharp, heavy claws, the Great Crab cut at the giant's legs until the water turned red. Little did she know that the giant was Hercules, and he dragged her up from the depths and crushed her against a rock with his mighty foot before killing the Hydra.

Hera had not wanted Hercules to succeed, and she was furious that he had killed her Great Crab. So she put new stars in the sky, creating a constellation. The Romans gave it the Latin name for crab: *Cancer*.

Did you know?
The slaying of Hydra was one of the Twelve Labours of Hercules – his second, in fact. Turn the page to read all about these labours, and the very first one Hercules faced. . .

LEO

SEASON: Around 23rd July until around 22nd August

Constellation　Symbol　Element

◇ Leo Star Sign Traits:
- Brave, confident and honest.
- Good at decision-making and leading the way.
- Proud, and affectionate to those who admire them.

Leo means 'lion' in ancient Greek, and lions were the most fearsome beasts known to the storytellers of old. In Greek art, the Lion appears wherever Hercules does — and here is the story of how that came to be.

Hercules was a son of Zeus who had superhuman strength but lived as a mortal. The goddess Hera cursed him with a fit of rage that caused him to murder his family. The king of his land ordered Hercules to earn forgiveness by completing twelve 'labours', all thought to be impossible.

The first task was to kill a lion, and not just any lion. Prized by hunters, this lion was famous for being able to kill all who approached him. His golden coat was magical — even the surest arrows and sharpest swords bounced off harmlessly. But Hercules did not know this. The king gave him thirty days to find the lion, kill him and bring back his hide.

Hercules searched until he found the bones and weapons of past warriors scattered on the ground, and heard the lion's deep growl nearby. Confident of his skills as an archer, he dared the lion to kill him. The huge lion appeared, and Hercules learned very fast that his arrows were useless. He found himself wrestling with the beast. Using all of his might, Hercules defeated the lion with his bare hands.

Even when he had killed the lion, he found that its magic hide could not be cut with a mortal blade. In vain Hercules struggled, until the goddess Athena came to his aid and told him to use the lion's own claw instead.

Hercules presented the lion's hide to the king the next day. The king was so impressed that he gave the hide to Hercules, who wore it always to protect himself from the arrows and swords of his enemies.

◇ **Virgo Star Sign Traits:**
• Thoughtful and observant.
• Sometimes reserved.
• Loves figuring out how to do things just right.
• Cool-headed and interested in the details.

VIRGO

SEASON: Around 23rd August until around 20th September

Constellation   Symbol   Element

The story of Virgo begins in a time when the gods, and all who lived under their protection, enjoyed a Golden Age. The Sun shone brightly, the rains fell generously, the crops grew heavy, and farm animals were plump and healthy. People enjoyed rich feasts and lived peaceably.

The goddess Virgo descended from a line of goddesses who embodied divine justice. Also known as Astraea or Dike, she lived on Earth, deciding disputes by weighing them up on her scales of justice. She enjoyed mortal company. In turn, she was celebrated for her gentle ways and her ready laughter. She was known as a true innocent: untouched by pain and a stranger to cruelty.

But people got used to life being easy and good, and they became greedy. They began to prize wealth above laughter and generosity. As selfishness replaced kindness, people who had once been friends turned on each other. Terrible wars began, and soon the lands were poisoned with blood. No crops grew and people had to fight each other just to get enough food to survive. The Golden Age had come to an end.

Horrified, Virgo sought refuge from humanity and fled to the skies, where she could watch over the world and issue her divine justice without being drawn into the chaos below. Virgo's constellation watches over all, her pure nature protected by the distance between heaven and Earth.

Did you know?
Virgo's passion for justice was inherited from her mother, the goddess Themis — who embodies the next star sign in this zodiac, known as Libra. Turn the page to find out more. . .

LIBRA

◇ **Libra Star Sign Traits:**
- Treats different points of view fairly.
- Particular and attuned to life's little pleasures.
- Gentle, favouring harmony above all.

SEASON: Around 21st September until around 23rd October

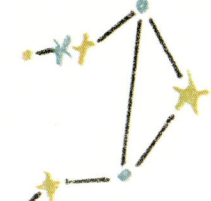  

Constellation   Symbol   Element

The constellation of Libra shines close to that of Virgo, and their stories are intertwined. Libra's constellation is linked to the autumn equinox, when daylight hours are equal to the dark, north of the equator. Around 3,000 years ago, the Babylonians named this constellation 'the Balance of Heaven', noticing its resemblance to an evenly weighted scale. Around the same time, many thousands of kilometres away, Chinese astronomers named these stars 'the Celestial Balance'.

The association with balanced weighing scales continued in ancient Greece, in the story of the goddess Themis, who was Virgo's mother.

Themis established fairness in the world early on in the time of Zeus. She was a powerful oracle who, being able to see the future, had the gift of prophecy. She wielded the sword of justice and, like Virgo, held weighing scales that could determine the right course of action in any dispute.

In the time before law existed, Themis was worshipped by all who had been wronged. It was said that night and day, her eyes were on the deeds of humans, and no evil action escaped her notice. Victims of theft and the families of those who had been murdered travelled from all over Greece to visit the Temple of the Oracles at Delphi. There they made sacrifices to Themis, and from on high, she applied divine law to their cases. The goddess Nemesis upheld all of Themis' laws by punishing those who broke them.

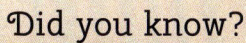

Did you know?
Themis and her descendants have been blended into a single icon of justice ever since. Next time you see a court of law, look around: a statue of her, blindfolded and holding her perfectly balanced scales of justice, may well be present.

◇ **Scorpio Star Sign Traits:**
- Values precision in all things.
- Relishes emotional highs and lows.
- Quiet and alert, and can be suspicious of others.

SCORPIO

SEASON: Around 24th October until around 21st November

Constellation   Symbol   Element

The goddess Artemis was a skilled hunter who presided over wild beasts and woodland glades. She liked to hunt deer in the moonlight, accompanied by divine nymphs who rejected the company of men. Artemis protected women when they were loyal to her, but was also known to curse her followers. She preferred to inspire awe rather than love.

Meanwhile, a son of the sea-god Poseidon grew up to become a giant — one with a legendary talent for hunting. His name was Orion, and though he was mortal, he could walk on water and was a hero among men. Orion carried a heavy bronze club, and was handsome, strong, and ruthless when it came to love. After breaking the heart of a mortal girl, he took up with Eos, the goddess of dawn. Then he turned his attentions to Artemis and her nymphs, but they wanted nothing to do with him.

Orion was frustrated. He decided to humble Artemis by besting her in doing what she loved most — hunting. Declaring that he would kill every living animal, he managed to enrage the Earth goddess, Gaia, who sent forth a gigantic scorpion. The scorpion stung Orion's heel, and he died.

Both Orion and the scorpion are preserved in the stars, eternally in battle. Scorpio is one of the largest constellations in the night sky, stretching across the Milky Way. It brightens in the autumn skies, just as Orion fades.

Did you know?
Scorpio was first recorded in the star maps of Mesopotamia, where its symbols translate as 'the creature that stings'. This means that scorpions have been linked to this group of stars for around 5,000 years.

SAGITTARIUS

SEASON: Around 22nd November until around 20th December

The name Sagittarius comes from the Latin word for 'arrow' — *sagitta* — and the story of this zodiac constellation is about an archer.

The stars that make up The Archer were first described in Mesopotamia, where a war god named Nergal was seen in the constellation. He was lord of the Sumerian underworld and, with his bow and arrow, was associated with death. Nergal was sometimes depicted with the powerful legs and cloven hooves of a goat.

In Greek mythology, The Archer of the stars was Krotos, a satyr with the head and body of a man and the hindquarters of a goat. Unlike Nergal, he lived on Earth, up on a mountain where many sacred springs jewelled the sunlit slopes.

Krotos rode a horse and tended sheep that lived on the mountain, using his skills in archery to protect the flock from wolves. He befriended three Muses who lived in the forests. The three Muses embodied Thought, Song and Memory, and together they appreciated creativity in all its forms. They liked Krotos' company, and decided to present him with a laurel garland that inspired poetry and music in him. After that he often drummed tunes for them to dance to.

Krotos admired the Muses in return, and he found their singing so beautiful that he brought his hands together, clapping to celebrate them. It is believed that, by doing so, he invented applause. As a reward, the Muses asked Zeus to put his image in the night sky, and so he became the constellation we now call Sagittarius.

Constellation

Symbol

Element

◇ **Sagittarius Star Sign Traits:**
- A free spirit who seeks out new horizons.
- Full of laughter and fun to talk to.
- Restless and easily bored.

CAPRICORN

◊ **Capricorn Star Sign Traits:**
- Persistent, and does not give up when things get difficult.
- A leader who cares about the people around them.
- Expects great things from life and aims for perfection.

SEASON: Around 21st December until around 20th January

Constellation   Symbol   Element

Capricorn takes the form of a sea-goat, a mythical being that has lived in the imaginations of astronomers since the ancient Middle Eastern empire of Babylon, many thousands of years ago. Astronomers saw the 'goat-fish' in the night sky as a symbol of their god of water and knowledge, Enki.

One thousand years later, the ancient Greeks gave the name Capricornus to this constellation, meaning 'horned goat'. Distant and faint, the stars that make up Capricornus are close to Aquarius and Pisces, two signs that feature water. The part of the galaxy they exist in is called The Sea, continuing the aquatic theme for this otherwise-earthy goat.

The Capricorn star sign has its own story: that of the Greek god Pan. Pan was cheerful and stubborn, and had boundless energy.

He was god of the wild groves and pastures, and played a special pipe made of reeds to tempt others to join him in having as much raucous fun as possible.

He was skilled in transformation and loyally helped Zeus win a great battle with the fearsome cave-dwelling serpent Typhon, whose very breath was fire and poison. Pan made himself into a goat and transformed the rubble around Typhon's cave into a tempting banquet of gleaming fish. This distracted Typhon's many snake heads and allowed Zeus to strike the monster with mighty thunderbolts.

But one of Zeus' thunderbolts went astray and hit Pan, who was killed alongside the monster. The gods put Pan in the stars in the form of Capricorn (half-goat, half-fish) to honour him for his ingenuity and service.

AQUARIUS

SEASON: Around 21st January until around 18th February

In the stars, the Aquarius constellation takes the form of a young man pouring water into the open mouth of a fish. This fish is part of Pisces, the constellation closest to Aquarius. But who was the young water-bearer?

A beautiful boy named Ganymede grew up in the ancient city of Troy. Born into a royal family, he was a prince, but he had no desire for luxury or wealth. He wanted to live a simple life. He decided to choose his own path and left the city to live on a leafy mountainside. There, he hunted stags with a javelin and cared for a flock of sheep with the help of his trusty dogs.

One sunlit afternoon, Ganymede was daydreaming as his sheep grazed nearby. A mighty eagle soared overhead and saw the lovely youth drowsing in the sun. The eagle was astonished by the boy's otherworldly good looks and wanted to gaze upon him forever. The eagle was Zeus, and he snatched Ganymede up and flew him away to Mount Olympus, careful to hold the boy's arms tenderly in his fierce claws so that his perfection would not be harmed.

Once Ganymede arrived in the Hall of the Gods, he was given the task of bringing the gods their refreshment. He was the most beautiful water-bearer the gods had ever seen.

Ganymede's dogs remembered their lost master and searched for him in the shadows of passing clouds, barking in the vain hope that he might hear them. Up on Mount Olympus, Zeus gave Ganymede eternal life to keep him forever young and immortalised him in the stars as Aquarius.

◇ **Aquarius Star Sign Traits:**
- Cares about making the world a better place.
- Clever, open-minded and willing to experiment.
- A creative spirit who inspires others.

Constellation

Symbol

Element

PISCES

SEASON: Around 19th February until around 20th March

Constellation   Symbol   Element

◇ **Pisces Star Sign Traits:**
- Has an imaginative, romantic nature.
- Kind, and cares deeply about other people.
- Likes to go with the flow but can find themselves adrift.

The nine stars of the constellation named The Fishes, or Pisces, were said by Babylonians to depict two fish tied together by a ribbon. Vedic astronomers of India associate this sprawling sideways V of stars with Vishnu, a vital god in Hinduism who is present everywhere, protecting all that is good. It is one of the largest constellations in the sky.

The idea of the two fish connected by a ribbon has travelled through time, from Mesopotamia and ancient Greece into the present. In the Greek myth, the two fish represent Aphrodite, the goddess of love, and her son Eros, the mischievous god-youth who sparked love between mortals by firing golden arrows into their hearts.

When the terrible serpent monster Typhon attacked Mount Olympus, he hoped to kidnap Aphrodite. She was afraid of Typhon, and ran with Eros to the banks of the River Euphrates, which winds through the countries we now call Turkey, Syria and Iraq. Aphrodite and Eros sought refuge among the tall reeds and rushes at the river's edge, hoping that they were well hidden.

But Typhon was determined to catch Aphrodite. He sent bandits to the river, and when Aphrodite heard them rustling in the reeds close by, she and Eros waded into the waters and prayed that the river nymphs would come to their aid. Two silver-scaled fish appeared in the water before Eros and Aphrodite, and went underneath them. The fish carried the two gods downstream, saving them from Typhon.

When Aphrodite and Eros reached safety, the people who welcomed them vowed never to eat fish again, and told the story of the two fishes whenever they looked up at the stars which bear their name.

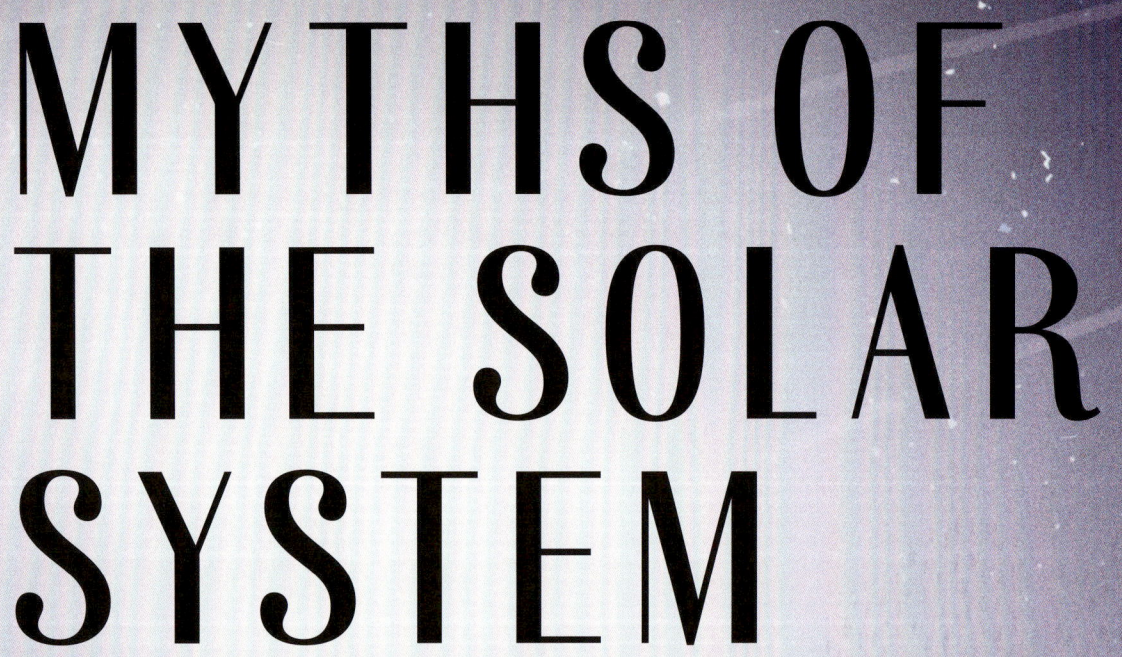

MYTHS OF THE SOLAR SYSTEM

Most of our solar system is pure emptiness. Vast, almost unthinkable distances stretch between the eight planets that orbit our Sun. But in the grand scheme, our entire solar system is just a dot, flung out on one of the four gigantic arms of a spiral galaxy — one of billions in our universe. And even further into the dark, whole other universes exist.

People have always felt awe when looking at the planets, even before we knew they were anything other than unusually colourful stars. Myths about them emerged over millennia, bringing these faraway worlds a little closer to us.

In this chapter, we will look at planetary myths from a range of folklore traditions — some from Europe, by way of ancient Rome; some from Latin America; and some from Africa. Each of these myths is associated with the major celestial bodies of our own little cosmos. Let's begin with a myth about our closest star: the ever-burning Sun.

Many of the myths in this chapter are based on Roman myths. This is because, in countries influenced by European culture, astronomers named the planets after ancient Roman gods and goddesses. However, most of these myths were based on ancient Greek myths to begin with! Read on to find out more...

THE SUN

The centre of our universe

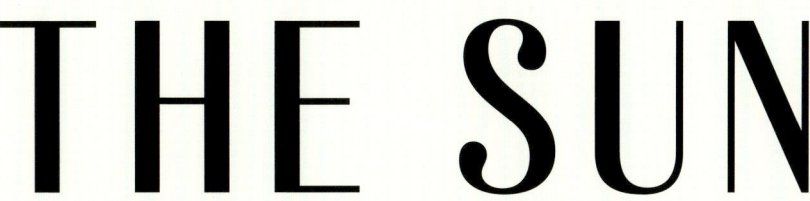

Star   Symbol

The Sun is more than four billion years old and has accompanied us at every stage of human evolution. It is the oldest-known object that any of us will ever see and is respected, admired and even worshipped around the world. Scientists predict that it will burn bright for another five billion years.

The Sun's light and heat makes all life possible. Without its power, no plants would grow, no animals would exist – and we wouldn't be here, either! Humanity has thrived thanks to the Sun's steady presence, and every community has a story about how it came to be.

The San people of southern Africa have lived on their ancestral territories for more than 20,000 years. As a desert people, they have always respected the Sun. In San folklore, the Sun was once a man with an unusual power: he could make daylight just by lifting his arms up.

His armpits shone with a magical light that amazed everyone. When he yawned and stretched every morning, he lit the whole world and made it warm. But over time, he got older and older, and he was getting too tired and stiff to stretch very much. The world began to get darker.

One day he slept for so long that everybody else got very cold without his light. A group of mischievous children crept up on him, and before he woke up to know what was happening, they grabbed him by the arms and legs and tossed him high up into the sky. The shining magic in him began to work again, and he transformed in the air, becoming a disc of pure light. He felt wonderful, endlessly strong and full of powerful heat. He became the Sun. His warmth and light has nourished the world and all its plants, animals and people ever since.

In ancient Greek mythology, the god Helios drove a chariot led by winged horses across the sky, with the Sun as his divine cargo. In the morning, he rose in the east, bringing dawn. At night he came to Earth in the west, bringing sunset, followed by the night.

MERCURY

The smallest, swiftest planet

Rock

Symbol

Little grey Mercury is closer to the Sun than any other planet and is only slightly bigger than our Moon. Small, dense and made of rock, Mercury speeds around the Sun in just eighty-eight Earth days.

In ancient Roman mythology, Mercury was the messenger god. Like the planet, he was faster than anyone else, thanks to his winged helmet. Nimble, young and clever, he often amused himself by playing tricks on mortals and monsters.

Mercury knew many, many stories because he remembered everything that the gods told him in their messages to each other. He also played pipes and sang. All this came in very handy one day when Jupiter, the god of the sky and thunder, called on Mercury for help...

Though married to Juno, the goddess of war, Jupiter had fallen in love with Io, a young moon-goddess. Juno was furious when she learned of this, so Jupiter decided to hide Io from his wife by transforming her into a white cow. But Juno knew Jupiter's tricks and demanded to be given the pretty heifer as a gift. Jupiter didn't want trouble, so Io was sent to graze among Juno's cowherd, which was watched over by his wife's sentry: the hundred-eyed giant, Argus.

Jupiter turned to mischievous Mercury, asking him to find a way to rescue Io. Mercury agreed and went to the valley where the all-seeing Argus stood over the cattle, his hundred eyes never blinking.

Mercury was friendly to Argus and chatted to him as he would a fellow traveller. He told Argus endless stories, making each one duller than the last, only pausing to play him the most dreary songs he'd ever heard.

Bored by the messenger, Argus began to fall into a stupor, and Mercury sang on until every one of the monster's hundred eyes had closed in sleep. Quick as a flash, Mercury killed the slumbering giant, dashed to Io and made her human once more. His limitless knowledge and wily nature saved the day.

Did you know?
Mercury was an ancient Roman god, based on the ancient Greek god Hermes. Jupiter was based on Zeus, and Juno was based on Hera.

VENUS

Planet of rain, war and love

Rock

Symbol

Before we knew about planets, people around the world thought Venus to be an especially pretty star, often referring to it as the Morning Star. Venus is covered in fiery volcanoes, and is the hottest and brightest of all the planets in our solar system.

Maya skywatchers in ancient Mexico, Belize and Guatemala were the first to notice that this super-bright celestial object was unusual. Unlike other stars, it disappeared completely from view for eight nights. And this happened every 584 days.

For the Maya, this 'star' was Kukulkan, a mighty god who took the form of a feathered serpent. Kukulkan was revered because he protected warriors and predicted rains that replenished the sun-parched land, allowing precious corn to grow.

But how did the divine Kukulkan communicate with the Maya? How did he tell them when to prepare for war or for the sowing season? He told them through the skies.

Kukulkan's bright star – or rather, the planet Venus – was visible at dawn and at dusk. Maya astronomer-priests tracked Venus' movements with great care, counting down the 584 days until the final night, when Venus disappeared completely. Absent from the sky, Kukulkan was thought to descend into the Underworld, die and return to life again – when Venus reappeared at the dawn of the ninth day as the Morning Star.

Kukulkan's return signalled that the Maya were blessed by his life force and now was the right time for battle. A special ceremony gave thanks for this: Maya priests drew blood from their own ears and tongues to give to Kukulkan. They performed this ritual offering in the court of the Maya's mightiest pyramid-shaped temple.

The same temple is also where priests learned that rains were coming. Twice a year, when day and night were equal in length, shadows ran down the length of the temple, creating the shape of a huge snake. After this appearance from Kukulkan himself, downpours would follow.

The orbit of Venus lasts for 225 Earth days, but the 584-day (or year-and-a-half) cycle of it seeming to appear and disappear is caused by another phenomena: Venus takes eight nights to pass between Earth and the Sun, and it is the Sun's glare that makes it invisible to us.

EARTH

Our miraculous mother

Rock   Symbol

Earth is many things, but most of all it is home. For all of our explorations of our galaxy, it is still the only place that we know is capable of sustaining life as we know it.

In Earth's soil, tiny seeds become all kinds of food. In Earth's atmosphere, raindrops nourish towering trees which then exhale the oxygen we breathe. In Earth's oceans, clouds of microbes sustain gliding giants of the deep. Earth is full of variety, wonder and beauty.

Across the Andean mountain range of South America, the people who have lived there since the time of the Inca revere Earth as a goddess who appears in the eternal form of an elderly woman, wise and stooped over with age. Her name is Pachamama, which means 'Mother Earth'.

Long ago, Pachamama created the four principles of our world: water, earth, sun and moon. Some say that the Sun, Inti, is her child, while others claim that she created him to be her companion. Together, they made the first crops of corn and potato grow, and they were worshipped by the Inca as fertility deities.

Pachamama was said to live deep within the mountains. When Pachamama was angered or harmed, she would shiver, and her trembling caused earthquakes, floods and droughts. She could transform into a dragon and breathe fire into the forests, too. To keep her contented, Inca priests wrapped offerings of quinoa, corn and cocoa leaves into clay pots named challa, and placed these in sacred mountain caves for Pachamama and her animal creations to enjoy.

Today, worship of Pachamama continues in Peru, Bolivia and other places touched by the Andean mountains. Modern worship of Pachamama involves being respectful to the land, protecting it and restoring balance. This elder goddess teaches us that we cannot take without giving back and that an injury to the planet injures us all. Pachamama reminds us that everything is connected.

The ancient Greeks and Romans both saw Earth as feminine, too: for them, Earth was the almighty goddess Gaia. She created the mountains and oceans alone, then married the sky-god Uranus to bring the Sun, Moon and stars closer to land.

THE MOON

Friend, goddess and big round man

Rock

Symbol

The Moon is our closest celestial body. We see it brighten each month, become fully round and then fall back into shadows. This is called waxing and waning.

In both ancient Greek and Roman mythology, the Moon was a goddess named Selene. She wore a shining cape and a crescent headdress, and she rode a chariot pulled by winged horses across the sky. Selene fell in love with a mortal shepherd boy, Endymion, and she put him under an enchantment where he slumbered in the same mountain cave every night so that she could find him.

Selene has many Moon-goddess sisters around the world, as most cultures see the Moon as feminine — but not every culture.

In southern Africa, the San people see the Moon as a man. When the Moon-man gets fat, the envious Sun fears his rivalry and cuts away at the Moon's roundness until only a tiny sliver is left. The Moon asks the Sun to have mercy and leave a slim crescent for his children. Feeling calm again, the Sun agrees, and so next month, the Moon is able to grow fat once more.

Some Indigenous Australian traditions see the Moon in a similar light — as a big round man who escapes death. In one story, the Moon lets his wife and daughters do all the work. One day, they get fed up with him and chop bits off him each night while he sleeps, until eventually he disappears! To their surprise, after four days he comes back and slowly becomes fat again. Having survived death, the Moon curses everyone so that when they die, they stay dead — and only he can ever return.

MARS

The iron-hearted red planet

Rock   Symbol

Mars was first recorded by astronomers in Mesopotamia over 4,000 years ago. It's famous for having a rusty colour, caused by the high quantity of iron within its dust-dry soil. If you see a reddish-orange, untwinkling star in the night sky, you have in fact found Mars.

In ancient Roman mythology, this planet was 'the fiery sphere', and its association with toughness, bloodshed and conflict can be seen in tales of Mars, the Roman god of war.

Mars was divinely born, the son of Jupiter and Juno. He wore heavy bronze armour, armed himself with a spear and shield, and was known for his raging thirst for battle. Nothing better pleased him than bloody scenes of carnage between warriors. Some mortals saw him as a protector of those about to fight, while others feared his savagery.

But Mars was not immune to love, and he fell for the goddess Venus, who was his opposite in every way. She was peaceful, playful and did not enjoy causing harm to others. In fact, she found cruelty abhorrent. Venus much preferred to see mortals love each other, rather than kill each other. Still, she admired Mars because he was not afraid of his passionate feelings.

Venus and Mars became a couple, and he became more rational, realising that violence is not the only solution to conflict. Together, they symbolised a union between Love and War, and they named their daughter Concordia, meaning 'harmony'.

> **Did you know?** Mars was an ancient Roman god, based on the ancient Greek god Ares. Both were gods of war.

> For the Babylonian and Sumerian people of Mesopotamia, this distinctive red planet was Nergal, the god-king of all wars, and its colour signified blood.

JUPITER

The stormy, red-eyed supergiant

Jupiter is colossal. It is by far the biggest planet in our solar system. More than 1,000 planet Earths could fit within this gargantuan world. In fact, all eight of the other planets could fit inside Jupiter and not even fill it up. There would be space for all their moons as well!

Jupiter is the ancient Roman name for Zeus, and the planet and Zeus have a few things in common. Like Zeus, Jupiter has enormous power — its gravity keeps almost a hundred moons in orbit. Since its surface sparks with electricity, Jupiter is prone to throwing out bolts of lightning. And Jupiter is stormy, with an endless hurricane raging through its atmosphere. Through a telescope, this storm looks like a red circle against the orange, brown and white stripes of the gas giant. It even has a name: the Great Red Spot.

Of Jupiter's many moons, four are visible through an ordinary telescope, and these are also named after familiar figures from ancient myths: Ganymede, Europa, Io and Callisto. All four of them were loved by Jupiter, and tricked by him, too.

In every myth of Jupiter, he is the all-powerful King of the Gods. Many gods try to fight him, trick him and take his throne, but none ever rival his size and strength. The only way to be safe around the god of sky and thunder is to escape his notice, or be forever fixed in his protective orbit — like the four largest moons of Jupiter.

Gas

♃

Symbol

In ancient China, Jupiter was called the Wood Star. Astronomers studied its movements closely, and one, named Gan De, even identified one of its satellite moons with his naked eye on a clear summer's night — around 2,000 years before anyone else!

Did you know? Jupiter was an ancient Roman god, based on the ancient Greek god Zeus. Both were gods of sky and thunder.

SATURN

The seven-ringed planet

Gas   Symbol

The planet Saturn was first sighted by Babylonian astronomers in the Middle East thousands of years ago. They noticed its yellow glow moving slowly among the stars and named it after their god of sun and harvest, Ninib.

Saturn is a striking planet, thanks to its spectacular rings. These are rather like force fields, holding ice and dust in suspension around the planet's widest point. More than a hundred moons circle Saturn's yellow atmosphere, and many moonlets, too. Saturn is the slowest-moving planet, famous for taking nearly thirty Earth years to orbit the Sun.

This planet's slow-moving nature meant that it was named after the ancient Roman god of time, Saturn. Born to Gaia and Uranus, he mutilated his violent sky-god father and drove him away. Saturn then ruled over the cosmos with the goddess Ops by his side. But an oracle told him that he would be overthrown by one of his own children. Determined to keep his power and stop the prophecy from coming true, Saturn came up with a brutal solution: every time Ops had a baby, he forced her to give it to him, and then he ate it in one gulp. He was god of time, he reasoned, and time devours all things.

All this made Ops wretched with grief. When she was about to give birth once more, she tricked Saturn by giving him a stone wrapped up like a baby. He ate it whole, thinking it a newborn. Ops then secretly gave her real baby to Saturn's mother, the Earth-goddess Gaia, who raised the child on an island, far from her dangerous son. The baby that she hid away was named Jupiter.

Jupiter was exceptionally strong, even as a child, and when he became a man, he fought Saturn and forced him to vomit up his eleven siblings. Jupiter then defeated his father in battle and banished him, fulfilling the oracle's prophecy. He and his siblings became the immortal gods and goddesses, ruling over heaven and earth.

Eventually, Jupiter ended Saturn's banishment and made his ageing father the King of the Blessed Isles, a golden paradise where honoured mortals went after death. Romans celebrated this wise old Saturn as a bringer of harvests and gave a day of the week his name: Saturday.

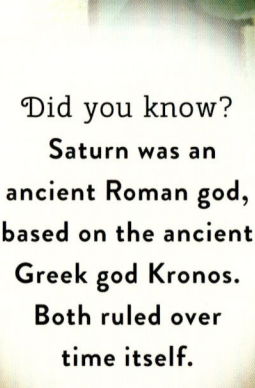

Did you know? Saturn was an ancient Roman god, based on the ancient Greek god Kronos. Both ruled over time itself.

Did you know? Saturn learnt to be brutal thanks to his father, the unloving sky-god Uranus. Turn the page to discover more about Saturn's troublesome creator...

URANUS

The chilliest planet in the cosmos

Ice

Symbol

Uranus is the coldest world in our solar system, despite being over 1.5 billion kilometres closer to the Sun than faraway Neptune. It is extra-cold because, early on in the development of our universe, Uranus was hit by a gigantic asteroid that knocked it from its upright position. This pale, blue-green planet and its twenty-eight moons have spun sideways ever since, and the Sun's rays barely reach its icy seas.

In ancient Roman mythology, Uranus was god of the sky. The planet was named after him because it was discovered many years after Saturn and Jupiter. In mythology, Uranus is Saturn's father and Jupiter is Saturn's son. Astronomers decided that these three planets represented three generations of Roman gods: grandfather, father and son.

Married to Gaia, the goddess of the Earth, Uranus brought stars and rains and bright blue horizons close to Gaia's vibrant lands and oceans. Together, they created the cosmos. Uranus and Gaia then had eighteen children: twelve were divine gods, three were one-eyed giants and three were strange beings with 100 hands each!

Uranus only liked the twelve divine children and he rejected the other six, even though Gaia loved them all. Uranus tried to kill the six children he hated by burying them deep in Gaia's earth, forcing them back into her body. Sickened by Uranus' cruelty, Gaia asked the twelve remaining children to avenge their siblings.

Of the twelve, only Saturn heard his mother's plea. He confronted his father with a magical blade and wounded him badly. Wherever Uranus' blood fell upon the land and sea, new gods and goddesses sprang forth. Venus herself, the Roman goddess of love, was born through this magic.

Uranus retreated to the sky realm and did not come back. He had played his part in the creation of the world. The Romans built no temples in his honour and rarely spoke his name.

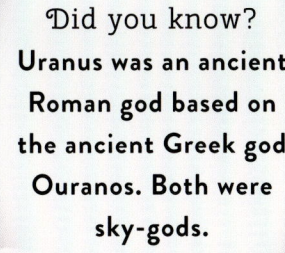

Did you know? Uranus was an ancient Roman god based on the ancient Greek god Ouranos. Both were sky-gods.

NEPTUNE

A distant deep-blue ocean world

Ice

Symbol

The Māori name for this oceanic planet is Tangaroa. In Māori mythology, Tangaroa is atua (god) of the sea, and he can take the form of a whale. He is the creator of all sea creatures.

Neptune is the most remote planet in our solar system, over five billion kilometres from the Sun. Dark and cold, it can only be seen through telescopes, which reveal its vivid blue colouring.

Neptune is covered by a vast sea that would seem very strange to us: the temperatures get so high that it produces zaps of electricity. At the same time, supersonic cyclones whip ceaselessly across it. These winds are so fast that they compress the seawater into a kind of hot, electrical ice-slush.

In ancient Roman mythology, Neptune was the god of all waters, and so this landless planet is named in his honour. Neptune wielded a three-pronged fishing spear — his trident — and rode over the seas on a chariot pulled by dolphin-tailed horses.

Neptune played a part in creating the evil-eyed Medusa, who was once an ordinary girl. She was one of three Gorgon sisters, and the only mortal one of them. Neptune took a liking to Medusa and went walking with her near the holy temple of Minerva, the goddess of wisdom. They strolled among Minerva's olive groves and listened to her owls hooting. In Minerva's sacred temple, Medusa rejected his advances, but Neptune ignored her.

This annoyed Minerva. She suspected that Neptune was insulting her because they had a long history of competing and outdoing each other.

The goddess decided to punish Neptune by transforming the innocent Medusa's long, fine hair into a writhing nest of venomous snakes. The goddess cursed Medusa's loving gaze, too: if she looked upon someone, they immediately turned to stone.

Though he was immortal and immune to her curse, fickle Neptune left Medusa, and she returned home broken-hearted. Luckily, her two immortal sisters were not at all afraid of her and taught her to enjoy the powers granted by Minerva's curse. In time, she became so fearsome that she forgot that she had ever been a mortal girl.

Did you know? Neptune was an ancient Roman god, based on the ancient Greek god Poseidon. Both ruled over the rivers, springs and seas.

PLUTO

The little planet that never was

When Pluto was first spotted a hundred or so years ago, it was thought to be the ninth and final planet in our corner of the Milky Way. That's because Pluto is round and luminous like a planet, and has five moons of its own.

But space exploration has since shown that Pluto is far smaller than it appears — much smaller than our own Moon — and is more of a spherical rock surrounded by many other similarly sized rocks. Pluto also has an irregular orbit, and so astronomers classify it as a dwarf planet.

This dark and distant space object was named after the ancient Roman god of the Underworld. Pluto was like his Greek counterpart, Hades, in that he was King of the Dead. His name means 'the unseen one'.

Today, Pluto's namesake in space is classified as a massive object, yet compared to the eight planets, it is tiny — to give you an idea of how small it is, Pluto could fit into the Pacific Ocean nine times over!

Pluto was brother to Jupiter and Neptune, and they were tasked with ruling over three realms — sky, water and the Underworld. Jupiter took the heavens, Neptune took the rivers and seas, and Pluto took the shadows. He preferred the peace of his subterranean kingdom to the stormy conflicts of the living world.

But he had a weakness — he wished to have a queen. He chose Proserpina, goddess of spring (known as Persephone in Greek mythology), but she didn't choose him. So he gave her a pomegranate, not telling her that every seed she ate represented a month of living in the Underworld. She ate six seeds before she realised his trick, but it was too late. At the end of every summer, Proserpina was forced to go into the world of the dead and be Pluto's Queen. The world became cold, dark and lifeless for six months until she returned, bringing spring with her.

Rock and Ice

♇ Symbol

Did you know? Pluto was an ancient Roman god, based on the ancient Greek god Hades. Both ruled over the dead.

MYTHS OF THE STARS

The night glitters above, pinpricked with light. Beyond the constellations of the Tropical Zodiac, every star in the night sky has a story — in fact, many have several. Over time, certain constellations and their individual stars have inspired lasting legends, and many different names.

Depending on where they live, people see stars in different positions, and they appear brighter in different seasons, too. Some star clusters inspire varied associations — a pattern that resembles an anchor for one storyteller looks more like a cross in the eyes of another. Yet some tales are similar around the world, evoking stories of siblings or bears in many different regions.

In this chapter, we venture into the cosmos one last time to explore a few amazing star stories from the Americas, Asia, Oceania, and western and southern Africa, among other places.

Did you know? Across time and different cultures, the Milky Way has had many names, including Star's Road, River of Heaven and The Place Where Lightning Rests.

THE MILKY WAY

A Band of Light

On dark nights, in places far away from city lights, a bright arc of stardust and stars can be seen stretching across the sky above us. This is the Milky Way, the part of our galaxy visible from Earth, and its beauty is a source of awe and delight around the world. Once seen, it is never forgotten.

Many myths of the Milky Way come from people who live in the southern hemisphere because its stars are extra vivid in southern skies. In some traditions, the stars in the Milky Way represent ancestors who have gone before us, and now look over us. In other traditions, they tell a story.

For the San people of the Kalahari desert in southern Africa, the Milky Way came to be when a young girl wanted to eat the roasted roots her mother was cooking in a fire. 'They smell so good! I want to taste them!' the little girl said, and despite her mother trying to stop her, she grabbed the roasting roots from the flames. The girl's hands were burnt by the roots and ashes, so she flung them up into the sky, scattering them. The embers of the roots became stars, and the fire's ashes became the hazy stardust of the Milky Way.

Though the Milky Way is as big as the sky itself, it's not always visible due to modern light pollution. Even a little bit of moonlight can make the galaxy less bright to us. To see the Milky Way as clearly as our ancestors might have seen it, you'd want to travel to the middle of an ocean, the middle of a desert or the top of a remote mountain.

SIRIUS

A Shining Mystery

The brightest of all the stars, Sirius, has captivated people for millennia with its luminous blue-hued twinkle. Appearing in the south in the mid evening, it has served as a valuable navigation tool, enabling seafarers who have lost their way by day to course-correct by night.

Far from the ocean, among steep red cliffs that loom over a sandy plain in Mali, West Africa, live people who revere Sirius for other reasons.

They are the Dogon people, and they practice a way of life that has existed for centuries, living in villages of tall red-earth houses that look out from the cliff faces. Every sixty years, Sirius appears between two mountains: a once-in-a-lifetime occurrence that the Dogon celebrate with a festival. They also observe the movements of Sirius' tiny companion star, a 'white dwarf'. This star is almost impossible to see, and western astronomers only discovered it quite recently — yet the Dogon have always been aware of it.

This is because Dogon people across the generations have shared a legend of how humanity came to be on Earth, thanks to these twinned stars. In the myth, the two stars are home to the Nomma: soft, aquatic water spirits. One of these spirits left their home star, the tiny white dwarf. They travelled across the heavens, standing on a square patch of sky. The water spirit arrived on Earth, the home of Amma, a creator god. There the Nommo created water. The Nommo was Amma's first living thing, and all Dogon people descend from spirit of the Sirius star system.

Many have disputed this myth, saying that that no one can be descended from star creatures. But the people of the red cliffs have centuries-old ceremonies revolving around the movement of Sirius and the companion star that no one else knew about. . . so who can really say?

The name Sirius comes from the Latin for 'scorching'. This super-bright star is twenty-five times more luminous than the Sun itself, and exists far away in a solar system beyond ours.

URSA MAJOR

The Great Bear

In Mesopotamia, the seven stars of Ursa Major were likened to the ploughs that farmers used to prepare their fields for planting season. 'The Plough' is a common name for Ursa Major today, particularly in Britain and Ireland. In the United States, it is known as the 'Big Dipper' because it resembles a ladle.

The constellation named Ursa Major represents a bear in many folk traditions, whether it is seen from the Great Plains of North America, the wind-shaped dunes of Mongolia or the sunny shores of the Mediterranean. In ancient Greece, the tale told about Ursa Major went like this. . .

A lonely princess of the forested vale of Arcadia went walking one day. Her name was Callisto. She came across a band of hunters, proud women who wore simple clothes and plaited their hair with white ribbons. Artemis, the goddess of the hunt, was their leader. Yearning for friendship and adventure, Callisto chose to join them and live in the wilderness. She and Artemis fell in love, and they hunted together side by side.

But the god Zeus (known as Jupiter in Roman mythology) wanted Callisto for himself. A powerful shape-shifter, he tricked her by appearing in the form of Artemis. By the time Callisto realised that she had been deceived, it was too late. Some months later, Artemis saw that Callisto was pregnant and banished her.

The goddess Hera, Zeus' wife, eventually discovered that her husband had given Callisto a child, a boy named Arcas. Furious, Hera turned her anger on Callisto and cursed her. The next day Callisto woke up to find that she had heavy paws instead of hands and feet, a long snout instead of her round face, and warm brown fur all over her body. She had become a bear.

She roamed the forests for years, hiding from hunters. One day, she saw her son Arcas walking through the woods, hunting deer with a bow and arrow. He had grown into a fine young man. Callisto was delighted to see him, and she ambled towards him, forgetting that she was a bear and he was a hunter. He prepared an arrow to shoot her with, but Zeus intervened, and swept his former lover and their son up into the stars, making them into constellations.

Though Callisto had little luck on Earth, for skywatchers she is beloved as one of the most recognisable constellations of the northern hemisphere.

YACANA

The Llama Spirit

In the high peaks of the Andes, the Milky Way appears to skywatchers as a wide, white river in the night sky. To the ancient Inca who lived here around 500 years ago, this sky-river mirrored one on Earth that wound through the valleys of their empire.

The Inca particularly noticed the dark cloud constellations within the Milky Way — the shadowy gaps between the bright stream of stars and stardust. These dark patches have distinctive shapes that remind people of their most important and beloved animals. In the Andes, one animal in particular can be seen in the darkness between the stars: the long, shaggy form of a llama.

Llamas have been cherished by people in the Andes for thousands of years. Today, Quechua people (descendants of the Inca) continue to live alongside llamas. They are an essential form of transport, easily carrying water, food and other essentials along steep mountain paths, and their thick woolly fur is used to make blankets and rope.

The eternal spirit of all llamas is nestled in the Milky Way as a patch of night between the stars, and her name is Yacana.

Her eyes are stars, and her long neck enables her to drink from any spring she chooses. She is accompanied by her Baby Llama, a smaller dark cloud constellation beneath her.

Every day, Yacana walks alongside the white river of the Milky Way and comes down to Earth at midnight when nobody is looking. Then she drinks all the waters of pain and sadness — the tears of the world. This is her task, and without her, the oceans and rivers would rise and rise until the world and all its creatures were drowned.

When her task is complete, she returns to the sky, and as dawn comes, her woolly coat appears streaked with many beautiful colours.

Did you know? Long ago, it was said that Yacana would rest upon a sleeping person at night and warm them with her soft, thick fur. On waking, the person would find that they'd been blessed with good fortune.

HIKOBOSHI AND ORIHIME

Star-crossed Lovers

On one the edge of the Milky Way, a bright star shines in the black. In Japanese folklore, it is known as the 'Boy Star' and represents the simple cowherd, Hikoboshi. According to legend, he fell in love with a princess, whose own star lies on the other side of the Milky Way.

Hikoboshi lived on one bank of this cosmic river of stars. The princess lived on the far bank, in the realm of the sky king, her father. She was called Orihime, and she was a skillful weaver. She loved nothing more than spending hours at her loom, making shimmering cloth out of stardust.

One day Hikoboshi and the princess saw each other across the star-river. They fell in love and married in secret. They quickly forgot about everything but each other. Hikoboshi let his cattle roam wild across the heavens. Orihime stopped weaving, preferring to gaze across the river whenever she had to spend time away from her love.

The sky king loved his daughter and was confused by her loss of interest in her beloved loom. But when he discovered her marriage to Hikoboshi, he was furious, and forbade her from ever seeing the cowherd again. The king hoped Orihime would return to weaving, but instead she followed him around, pleading that he change his mind. Finally, he agreed, and declared that Orihime could see Hikoboshi for just one day each year.

A year passed and the first meeting day arrived, but the lovers found the Milky Way river to be too wide and deep to cross. Orihime cried so loudly that a flock of magpies came and used their wings to make a bridge for her, and the lovers were able to be together again.

In Japan, the union of these star-crossed lovers is celebrated each year on the seventh day of the seventh month, when Orihime's star is brightest. This is Tanabata, or the Star Festival, and like Valentine's Day, it's dedicated to lovers. It is said that if it rains on festival day, the magpies stay away. But if the skies are clear, the magpies return and Hikoboshi and Orihime are reunited.

The folktale of a cowherd and a weaver girl has been told for thousands of years in China, too. This popular tale of forbidden love was first recorded in a poem that is more than 2,600 years old. The story is celebrated today on Qixi, or the 'Double Sevens': the seventh day of the seventh month.

MĀUI'S FISH HOOK

The Origin of Hawai'i

For ancient astronomers in the deserts of the Middle East, the downward-curving tail of Scorpius reminded them of scorpion tails, ready to sting. Yet these same stars look very different upside down, as they appear when seen from tropical islands in the southern hemisphere. Here, they seem to curve upwards, resembling the traditional fishhooks that Polynesian people use to catch their fish.

In Hawai'i, these stars are called Māui's Fish Hook. Māui was a mythical hero who lived long ago. He was famed for his love of fishing — and his lack of skill with it. He could often be found casting his line out over the beautiful coral reefs that surrounded the lone mountain that made up his island home. His four brothers, all skilled fishermen, liked to ask him if he'd caught anything. He never had, and his brothers always had a good laugh at Māui's expense.

One day, Māui went with his brothers on a fishing trip out on the ocean. Māui brought a magical fish hook with him, which he'd lovingly made from a jawbone that had once belonged to his grandmother. He cast the magic hook into the water and down it sank. He felt a great tug, and he asked his brothers to paddle forwards and not look over their shoulders.

The brothers paddled and paddled, and Māui used all his strength to pull up what he'd caught. First came rocks, then came land, trees and mountains. A whole new island rose from the waves. Another island followed, and another — eight in total. But one of Māui's brothers stopped paddling, and looked over his shoulder, and no more islands came after that. The eight islands that Māui's magic fish hook had caught became the nation of Hawai'i.

Did you know?
Māui's fishhook can be found in the Milky Way, close to a dark patch of the sky — a dark cloud constellation, in fact. This dark shape is known in Hawai'i as the 'Fish Leaping in the Shadows'. The hook appears at the front of this fish shape, as if it is pulling this celestial catch across the night sky.

The Seated Queen

CASSIOPEIA

In the northern skies, five bright stars form the shape of the letter 'W'. This distinctive asterism was seen as an antlered stag by Babylonian skywatchers of Mesopotamia — but for the ancient Greeks, these stars tell the story of a queen who fell foul of a god.

Cassiopeia was Queen of Ethiopia in East Africa, and she was famed for her supernatural beauty. People who saw her lost track of their thoughts, forgot who they were and rushed to do her bidding. Because her looks so enchanted everyone, she never had to ask for anything twice, and she was proud that she never used force to rule over her subjects. She was also proud of her daughter, Andromeda, who was as gorgeous as she was.

One day, Queen Cassiopeia looked out to sea and saw the immortal Nereid sea nymphs gliding in the waves. Like her, the Nereides were beautiful, but they ruled over no one but themselves. 'I have more power than them, and so does my darling Andromeda,' said Cassiopeia.

'It must be because we are more beautiful than they are.' She asked the people of her court what they thought, and as usual they fell over themselves to agree with her.

The god of water, Poseidon, overheard Queen Cassiopeia's musings. He disliked hearing the Nereides be criticised by a mere mortal, even if she was a queen. He thought Cassiopeia was far too proud and decided to punish her. He knew that Cassiopeia loved her daughter above all, so he chained Andromeda to a sea cliff and sent a monstrous whale to devour her. Then he banished Cassiopeia to the stars, where the gods bound her to an upside-down throne with a mirror in her hand to symbolise her vanity. Yet some say that she ignored the mirror, and preferred to watch over her lost lands instead.

But what of Andromeda? The heroic god Perseus was flying on his winged horse, Pegasus, when he saw a sea monster lunging towards her. He released her from Poseidon's chains and the two fell in love. When her long and happy mortal life came to an end, Perseus made sure that Andromeda joined her mother in the stars, where their constellations sit side by side for eternity.

THE WAYFINDER'S FRIEND

Icon of the southern skies

Centuries ago, an Italian navigator voyaged across the southern seas and wrote many letters home to describe the amazing things he saw. When he witnessed the five stars of the Crux constellation, he wrote that their pattern was "so fair and beautiful that no other heavenly sign may be compared to it".

Found in the Milky Way, Crux is the smallest of the eighty-eight internationally recognised constellations. Though tiny, it is exceptionally bright and is perhaps the most widely beloved constellation of the southern hemisphere, featured on the national flags of Brazil, Aotearoa, Papua New Guinea, Samoa and Australia.

Across different cultures, Crux is associated with a number of things due to its distinctive shape. These include a bird's footprint, a flying kite, a grain store, a spinning top and an anchor. It's also easy to draw two lines between its four brightest stars to form a crucifix, the symbol of Christianity. Because of this, Crux is widely known as the Southern Cross.

Christians aren't alone in seeing a cross in these stars. In the Andes mountains of South America, Quechua people see the shape of Chakana, a rounded cross named by their Inca ancestors. Chakana is the heavenly navel of the Inca universe. Its four main stars signify many important things, including fire, air, water and earth, and the four directions: north, south, east and west.

Crux's four directions have played a historic role for people navigating the southern seas. Early seafarers discovered that they could sail directly south by following the southernmost star. If you followed this course all the way, you would eventually reach Antarctica. The constellation never sets in the night skies of the southern hemisphere, making it a trusty guide from dusk 'til dawn.

The southernmost star of Crux's cross shape is called Acrux, and powerful telescopes have shown that it is in fact a triple star. These distant stars are 16,000–25,000 times brighter than the Sun.

Did you know? In a number of different cultures, Crux resembles a celestial stingray. The constellation is referred to as 'the ray stars' from the coasts of Australia to the islands of the Philippines, Indonesia and Malaysia, as far as Brazil.

ORION'S BELT

A Little Line

The story that the San and Xhosa people of southern Africa tell about these three stars concerns a girl who had rare magical powers. One day, she was playing on the savannah when she realised that a pride of lions was watching her from the long, golden grass. Her magic was so strong that, even though she was alone and the lions were hunting her, she felt no fear. When they began to run towards her, she simply transformed them all into stars. The three fiercest lions are the ones we see in this constellation today.

Three stars make an almost-straight line in the sky — almost, but not quite. The first two stars line up, but the third sits slightly off to one side. The trio make for a distinctive group, and are one of the easiest constellations to see at any time of year, from anywhere in the world.

The ancient Greeks named these three stars 'Orion's Belt', as they form the belt-like middle part of the much larger constellation of Orion, the hunter who was stung by a scorpion in the zodiac myth of Scorpio. Orion's constellation sits next to Scorpio in the sky, and he can be seen as an archer, eternally holding up his bow, ready to fire his next shot.

The ancient Greeks weren't the only ones to take inspiration from these three stars. The Aztec people of Mexico based one of their most sacred and brutal ceremonies on the stars of Orion's Belt, which they called 'Fire Drill'.

The ceremony required priests in the capital of the Aztec empire to keep a holy fire burning all day and all night for fifty-two years, until Fire Drill's three stars aligned with the horizon. This was seen as a symbol of a new era — but also a dangerous time when fearsome star-goddesses might come down to Earth and destroy everything.

To appease these goddesses, the holy fire was put out along with every other fire in the empire. In the darkness, people broke all of their old belongings and cast them into rivers, ready for a new beginning.

Then, at the top of a crooked hill at the city's edge, lit only by the stars themselves, the priests sacrificed a 52-year-old person who was deemed worthy of the goddesses. They then lit a new fire in the chosen person's body, using a holy stick decorated with an eagle's feather.

This deadly ritual was a way of reigniting the spark of life itself. When this once-in-a-generation New Fire Ceremony was over, people could begin again, relighting their own fires and giving thanks to the gods for new life.

THE FOUR STAGS

Nordic Star-deer

The Norse gave two stars special names — there was blóðstjarna, which means 'the bloody star', and morgunstjarna, 'the morning star'. They had in fact found the red planet, Mercury, and the dawn-rising planet, Venus.

In icy polar regions, stars share the night with a breathtaking phenomena called the aurora borealis. Immense shimmering ribbons of green, purple, pink and blue light dance across dark skies. Caused by electrically charged sun particles colliding with magnetised atoms, the aurora has amazed people for millennia as it dances through the stars.

The Norse story of how the stars came to be begins in the mythic branches of the World Tree, a mighty ash named Yggdrasil.

According to legend, Yggdrasil's roots spread as far as its branches — as far as the eye can see, and beyond. Within these spreading roots and branches were Nine Realms, and one of these was Muspelheim, a primordial region filled with fire. The Norse gods went to Muspelheim and gathered an array of burning sparks, which they placed in the night sky to create stars.

These stars were a mirror of the World Tree, forming patterns that revealed the Nine Realms. Few records of Norse constellations have survived, but the stars that represent four deer who lived in the World Tree's branches can still be found.

All four of the deer are young stags. They are Dáinn (the Dead One), Dvalinn (the Unconscious One), Duneyrr (Thundering in the Ear) and Duraþrór (Thriving Slumber).

In Norse lore, these fours stags eat the World Tree's leaves, and they collect dew upon their antlers every morning, which then flows into the rivers of the world.

The almost-forgotten star patterns of the four stags are clearest on deep, moonless midwinter nights in the northern hemisphere — but only when the bright dancing lights of aurora borealis are at rest.

Did you know? In both West Africa and Southeast Asia, the stars are known as the Mother Hen and her Chicks. In Japan the name for this cluster means 'to gather together'. In Aotearoa, these stars are called Matariki and their midwinter rising signals the Māori New Year, an occasion celebrated by spending time with loved ones.

THE SEVEN STAR-SISTERS

A Family of Stars

This cluster of stars has many names: Rain Stars, Seven Sisters, Daughters of the Night... Most stars in this group are too faint for us to see, but when the weather turns cold and rainy, six or seven can be reliably seen from anywhere on the planet. Storytellers and stargazers the world over have mapped myths and folklore onto this sparkling patch of the heavens.

For the ancient Greeks, the seven stars were the Pleiades (pronounced plee-ah-dees), a set of sisters. They were daughters of Atlas, a Titan who had gone to war with Zeus and whose punishment was to hold up the heavens on his shoulders for eternity. With their father out of the way, the hunter Orion set his sights on the sisters and wanted them as his lovers. The sisters were saved from this fate by Zeus, who rescued them by making them stars and placing them in the sky.

The Kiowa and Lakota peoples in North America know these stars to be sisters too. Their story goes like this...

Once upon a time, there were seven sisters who liked to play among the big boulders near their family's camp. One day, they disturbed an enormous bear who was sleeping nearby and he began to chase them. The sisters ran as fast as they could and called out to the Great Spirit for help. Frightened for their lives, the girls scrambled to the top of a huge boulder. The bear was close behind them.

Suddenly, the Great Spirit caused the boulder to grow tall, up and up and up into a huge tower. The angry bear tried to claw his way up the rock, but he could only scratch deep grooves into the sides. Safe in the sky, the seven sisters became stars. The tower of rock became known as Mato Tipila, which means Lodge of the Bears, and it's a place sacred to Kiowa and Lakota peoples. Each winter, the little cluster of star-sisters can be seen to dance above Mato Tipila once again.

No matter where the myths come from, nearly all of them associate these specific stars with siblings or the broader theme of family. And, centuries after these myths were woven, modern astronomers discovered something incredible: these stars are indeed related, having been born from the same cloud of dust and gas.

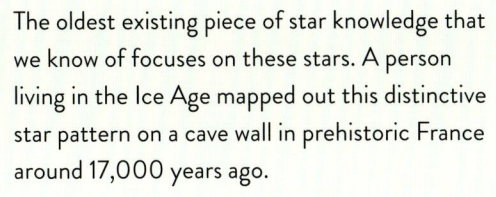

The oldest existing piece of star knowledge that we know of focuses on these stars. A person living in the Ice Age mapped out this distinctive star pattern on a cave wall in prehistoric France around 17,000 years ago.

STAR KNOWLEDGE AROUND THE WORLD

We have now explored the Tropical Zodiac in detail and learnt some of the myths and stories behind our planets and stars, but there's still a whole world of astrology stories and systems to discover.

This chapter explores the ways different countries and cultures have used and connected with the stars over the centuries, from cultures who relied on the stars to build calendars and travel the seas, to those who built their own zodiacs with their own symbols and stories . . .

A COMPASS MADE OF STARS

Wayfinding across the mighty pacific

The Pacific Ocean is the biggest ocean on the planet. It contains many islands that are thousands of kilometres away from the mainland in any direction. A ship can go for days in the Pacific and see only outcrops made of white sand and populated solely by seabirds. So, how did the earliest people come to live on islands surrounded by miles and miles of sea — places like Hawai'i, Tahiti and Aotearoa?

The answer is that the forebears of today's Māori and Polynesian peoples were exceptionally skilled. The only way to leave the Asian mainland was by invention and observation. Invention meant crafting wooden boats that could sail for weeks at a time, weathering every kind of oceanic storm. Observation meant learning to read the wind, the tides, the migratory patterns of birds — and the stars.

This method of navigation still exists today. A person who navigates a voyage in this way is known in Polynesian culture as a wayfinder. The wayfinder observes which constellations are rising from the ocean's horizon and, factoring in the wind and the currents, sets the boat's course in relation to this eternal map in the sky.

Each Pacific Island has its own star compass — a specific mental map, known by local wayfinders, that relates to the place they voyage from. A star compass does not exist as a physical object that can be bought and sold, like a nautical chart; it is remembered by people instead.

Wayfinding has survived for thousands of years against the odds. Elders teach young people how to read the subtle changes in the world around them, and tell them stories of voyages that live on as myths and lessons.

THE CITY CALENDARS OF THE MAYA

A civilisation planned by astronomers

A thousand years ago, Mexico, Guatemala and Belize were home to an advanced civilisation governed by astronomy: the ancient Maya.

Maya people lived in cities built in grids around towering, pyramid-shaped temples. Astronomer-priests designed these to act as monumental calendars, aligned with sunrise and sunset. These temples contained secret chambers and were carved with sculptures that cast special shadows on sacred days.

Maya astronomers also devised some of the earliest-known astronomical records and observatories, tracking the orbit of the planet Venus – known to them as a feathered serpent named Kukulkan. They noticed that Kukulkan would disappear from the night sky every 584 days. By observing both the skies above and the world around them, the Maya developed one of the most accurate calendar systems ever known.

There are three Maya calendars, all circular in design. The first is guided by the Sun. It contains exactly 365 days, and aligns with the Sun's movements and the growing season of corn. The second calendar, named the Tzolk'in, contains 260 days, or nine months – the same length of time as a typical human pregnancy. Priests used this calendar to plan spiritual customs such as naming ceremonies, the ritual cleansing of all households, and when to have weddings, holidays and initiations for new priests. The third calendar counts fifty-two-year eras – and predicts when the world will end!

The advanced nature of Maya astronomy is still admired by stargazers today, and its complex timekeeping system is still used by the descendants of Maya people. When a villager is planning a wedding, the planting of a crop or the beginning of a new enterprise, they'll ask their local shaman to consult the Maya calendars to find the luckiest, most sacred day possible.

Maya pyramid-temples conceal a sacred inner chamber that lies in darkness all year long until the summer solstice. On this day, the Sun reaches its highest point in the sky, aligning with the chamber's portal to the world outside. Each summer solstice, for just a moment, the sacred chamber fills with light.

Around 500 Inca priestesses lived in a special temple where no men could enter. They wove cloth, ground corn, and were treated with reverence by the townspeople. They were known as the Women of the Sun.

THE CHILDREN OF THE SUN

Sun worship among the Inca

The Inca empire was the last of of several great indigenous civilisations of the Andes, a mountain range that runs through South America: from Colombia, through Ecuador, Peru and Bolivia, all the way to Chile.

Much Inca culture was destroyed by Spanish colonisers, but ruins of some of their remarkable structures survived. These were holy temples, built at the top of towering mountains and dedicated to the worship of the Sun.

Inca people referred to themselves as the Children of the Sun. The emperor was responsible for predicting the seasons so that his people could grow plenty of maize and raise many llamas. Learned priests studied the Sun's movements for the emperor using gigantic sundials.

The most famous of these dials can be found in Peru, on the remote mountain peak of Machu Picchu, which is a series of ancient Sun temples, and one of the great wonders of the world.

When the Sun aligned with the sundials, there would be great feasts and llama sacrifices. Comets and star showers were considered lucky. Inca observed the bright band of stars that we now call the Milky Way and named it Mayu. Mayu was believed to be a sacred river and the source of all water on Pachamama, the Andean name for Mother Earth that is still used today. (To learn more about Pachamama, go to page 46.)

In Inca culture, the dark spaces between the stars — named yana phuyu, or 'dark clouds' — matter more than the stars themselves. The dark clouds are the constellations. They connect to stories about a llama shepherdess, a snake and a mother and baby llama, whose story is told on page 70.

THE AZTEC SUN SACRIFICES

When the Sun fed on blood

Hundreds of years ago, three great cities lay between the lakes and volcanos of northern Mexico and were populated by a people who came to be known as the Aztecs. Like the Maya before them, the Aztecs built huge pyramid-temples and worshipped many different gods. And like the Maya, they revered the Sun.

Aztec astronomer-priests believed that four different Suns had lived and died, and that they lived in the era of the Fifth Sun. When a Sun died, disaster followed. The first Sun era ended because the Sun was weak, and when the sky went black its god commanded a pack of jaguars to eat everyone who survived. In the next Sun era, people became too greedy, so the gods turned them into monkeys and banished them with a hurricane. In the third Sun era, the god in charge was distracted by heartbreak and forgot to send rain. When people begged him for water, he angrily sent rains of fire instead. The fourth Sun era ended when the goddess in charge cried for fifty-two years and caused a flood, and her people turned into fish in order to survive.

To keep the Fifth Sun strong, Aztec priests offered regular human sacrifices to the gods. The Aztecs had eighteen months in their year, and once each month, warriors brought a prisoner of war to the top of the pyramid-temple. There, the priests killed the prisoner by cutting out their heart, which they dedicated to Huitzilopochtli, their Sun god. They did this to ensure that the Sun and life-giving rains kept returning.

Aztec priests also planned far more elaborate and equally gory ceremonies. Some lasted for twenty days at a time; one lasted for an entire year. And every fifty-two years, when three stars appeared at the right place in the sky, all Aztecs took part in a ritual of blood and fire to prevent the end of the world. This was the New Fire ceremony, and you can learn more about it on page 80.

EMPERORS, ASTERISMS AND ECLIPSES

The wisdom of the stars

For almost 2,000 years, China was ruled by dynasties of all-powerful emperors. The success of each dynasty depended on the stars because good fortune on Earth came from the skies above. An unlucky comet could change everything for an emperor.

Astronomers lived at the Imperial Court in Beijing and studied the sky every night so they could predict the emperor's fortunes. The North Star was the emperor of the heavens, and the other stars reflected his kingdom below.

Over the centuries, court astronomers recorded more than 1,400 different stars in complex star maps, called planispheres. They also mapped 283 different asterisms, which are little groups of stars, smaller than constellations.

The sky was divided into four quarters: the Azure Dragon of the East, the Black Tortoise of the North, the White Tiger of the West and the Vermilion Bird of the South. These quarters divided again, into twenty-eight areas called mansions, which the Moon travels through.

The calendar developed by Chinese astronomers was lunar, meaning that it tracked the Moon's path. In fact, the rising and setting of the Sun and the waxing and waning of the Moon was seen as a great battle between opposing forces.

The emperor lived in fear of his astronomers informing him that the Moon would pass in front of the Sun, eclipsing the daylight. That was because a lunar eclipse was a divine message that declared the end of an emperor's rule. When such an eclipse occurred during the reign of the Qing dynasty Emperor Qianlong, he gave up the Imperial throne even though he had ruled China for sixty years.

THE CHINESE ZODIAC

A twelve-year calendar emerged from Chinese astronomy. It remains popular around the world, beloved for the twelve animals that represent each year. You are said to share the traits of the animal of the year you were born in. Which animal are you?

The Year of the…

Rat 鼠 — Imaginative and smart. You are sensitive and good at spotting opportunities. Years include: 1996, 2008, 2020.

Ox 牛 — Responsible and blessed with good judgement. You have natural leadership abilities. Years include: 1997, 2009, 2021.

Tiger 虎 — Brave and warm-hearted. You are determined and others admire your power. Years include: 1998, 2010, 2022.

Rabbit 兔 — Sweet-natured and mysterious. You can be shy around strangers, and affectionate with friends. Years include: 1999, 2011, 2023.

Dragon 龍 — Energetic and inspiring. You have many talents. Dragon is the luckiest animal of the Chinese Zodiac, and the only mythical one. Years include: 2000, 2012, 2024.

Snake 蛇 — Persuasive and quick-witted. You enjoy the finer things and value your independence. Years include: 2001, 2013, 2025.

Horse 馬 — Free-spirited and courageous. You attract many friends because you are respectful of others. Years include: 2002, 2014, 2026.

Goat 羊 — Kind and creative. You value quiet surroundings and peaceful friendships. Years include: 2003, 2015, 2027.

Monkey 猴 — You're likely to be an original thinker who gets into trouble easily and then charms their way out of it. Years include: 2004, 2016, 2028.

Rooster 雞 — Confident and organised. You like to get to the point and are good at making decisions. Years include: 2005, 2017, 2029.

Dog 狗 — Cheerful and enthusiastic. People know they can rely on you, and you often befriend others. Years include: 2006, 2018, 2030.

Boar 豬 — Optimistic and untidy. You tend to attract success and are naturally generous. Years include: 2007, 2019, 2031.

THE GREAT RACE

How the twelve animals were chosen

Once upon a time in China, the Jade Emperor decided that time should be measured in a twelve-year cycle. 'And each year will be named after an animal,' he thought. 'But which animals?' He announced a race: the first twelve to cross his river would win a place in the Chinese Zodiac.

Cat and Rat teamed up but were not strong swimmers. 'Let's ask kind Ox if we can ride on his back,' suggested Cat. And Ox was happy to let Rat and Cat ride across the river with him while he swam. But when they reached the far bank, Rat pushed Cat into the water and leapt on to dry land. Rat won the first zodiac year and Ox was given the second.

Tiger was powerful and saw no need to rush. Arriving just after Ox, he claimed third place.

Rabbit couldn't swim but found a way across by hopping on stones, then jumping on to a log that floated by. She was glad when the wind blew her to safely to shore, where the Jade King gave her the fourth zodiac year.

Dragon was slower than Jade Emperor expected. 'I saw a little rabbit floating on a log,' said Dragon. 'I stopped to blow a breeze her way so that she landed safely.' Dragon didn't mind being fifth.

Horse swam fast, eager to take the sixth zodiac year. But Horse hadn't noticed that clever Snake had coiled herself around one of his hooves. As they neared the river bank, Snake darted to shore, leaving Horse in seventh place.

Rooster, Goat and Monkey found a raft. They floated across together and the Jade Emperor thought them a fine team. He gave eighth place to Goat, ninth place to Monkey and tenth place to Rooster.

The Jade Emperor had expected eager Dog to win. But Dog enjoyed the fresh water of the river so much that he chose to bathe instead. He won the eleventh place.

The last to arrive was Boar. He had been too sleepy and hungry to swim, so he ate, then napped. After that, he swam very well. The Jade Emperor was happy that Boar was able to take the twelfth place in the zodiac.

Cat didn't get her place in the Zodiac, because Rat pushed her in the river. This is why cats dislike water — and why they enjoy catching rats!

ASTROLOGY TODAY

There is no single astrological story for what we see above us in the skies. And over time, myths and facts have been blended together, making our star stories bigger, more complicated and even more amazing.

A farmer in Mesopotamia once looked up at the stars and saw a plough similar to his own. Today, an astrophysicist can look up and see the exact same seven stars, only now she can tell you their names — Alkaid, Mizar, Alioth, Megrez, Phecda, Dubhe and Merak — and tell you what they are made of and even how many light years apart they are, too!

Astrology (the study of the celestial bodies above us and their movements) has become richer over time as well. Today, we use astrological star lore as a tool for understanding our personalities. And when we tell star stories, we remember myths that have been lovingly passed down through the generations, across time itself.

Before we go, let's take a quick look at astrology today. . .

ASTROLOGY AND ASTRONOMY

What's the difference?

Long ago, the word astrology was simply one way to describe the study of the Sun, Moon, planets and stars. Other words and phrases include stargazing, day keeping, skywatching, star knowledge and astronomy. If astrologers, astronomers, shamans, priests and day-keepers could have met across time and place, they would have had plenty to talk about!

Today, things are a little different: only the scientific observation of stars, planets and space as a whole is called astronomy. Today's astronomers predict eclipses, blue moons and meteor showers, just as astrologers once did. But technical explorations of space mean that today's astronomers also know a lot about the rocks, gases, dust and liquids that planets and stars are made from. An astrophysicist might dedicate their life to identifying new galaxies, or researching phenomena such as nebulas, black holes or supernovas.

Astrology today is still about paying attention to the stars and planets, but more focused on the idea that celestial bodies and their movements have a unique effect on our lives and personalities. According to astrology, the placement of the Sun, Moon and planets can influence who you are and what you do.

An astrologer uses their knowledge of zodiac constellations and planetary movements to help you figure out who you are and how to handle what's coming your way. Anyone can consult with a professional astrologer. They will consider your birth chart and provide you with a horoscope that suggests how your day, week or month may go.

In some astronomy circles, astrology is dismissed and seen as a distraction from hard science and reality. And astrologers don't necessarily care too much about the specifics of space – things like light years and the hydrogen composition of Jupiter's oceans.

Differences aside, astronomy and astrology share the same root: humanity's fascination with the night sky. In this way, they are like siblings — they may not always get along, but the studies remain very much related!

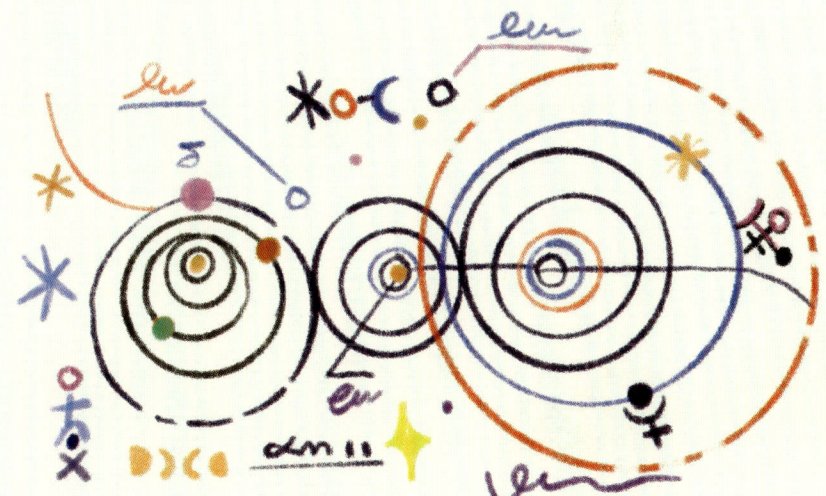

Each star within a constellation is of great interest to astronomers. For instance, the four brightest stars of the Crux constellation each have their own scientific profiles: α Crucis is a triple star, β Crucis is a blue-hued giant star, γ Crucis is a double star and δ Crucis is another blue-hued giant.

A KEY TO UNDERSTANDING

Astrology, star signs and you

Astrology is more popular in the modern world than ever before. We see astrology in the animals of the Chinese Zodiac that adorn Lunar New Year celebrations every year, and Tropical Zodiac astrology is easy to find all over the world online, in newspaper horoscopes and on birthday cards.

Star signs can come up in conversation wherever you go. Someone may be curious to know if you were born in the Year of the Horse, perhaps, or under the Sagittarius constellation of the Tropical Zodiac. Not everyone loves astrology, of course — within any big group of people, you'll find that some dismiss any kind of astrology as nonsense, others will see it as a bit of fun and some will take it quite seriously.

You can play with astrology by asking a friend about their star sign. It's a fun and easy way to get to know someone a little better and learn more about their specific sign. They may really enjoy their star sign and relate to the traits associated with it. 'I'm super Scorpio!' they might say. 'I like to plan ahead and take care of every detail.'

Or they may shrug and point out that their star sign is completely unlike them. 'I'm an Aries, but I'm not competitive at all,' they might say. 'I don't play sport much either. I'm more chill and into art!'

One thing is certain: the way a person feels about their star sign can give you a sense of who they are and how they think about life!

Based on what you know about the zodiacs and their signs, how do you feel about astrology today?

DEAR STAR SEEKER. . .

Your astrological journey is just beginning. Luckily, the stars, planets and moons of our universe are not going anywhere — not for millions and billions of years!

The many strange and wonderful myths and beliefs attached to the heavens above are there to be told, shared and remembered. We have only looked at a few of the great stories of the skies. If you enjoy them, there are more to be discovered. . .

Explore, too, your star signs in each of the great zodiacs and have fun with whatever you find.

Remember to always look up on the clear, dark nights, and take in the majesty of the cosmos. Gaze for long enough and you might see a shooting star!

Seeing the stars will remind you of the companionship of all the storytellers who came before us, the people who gave us the gift of seeing the night sky this way: as a sparkling and eternal parade of animals, ancestors, monsters, gods and spirits.

INDEX

A
Amma 66
Andromeda 77
Aotearoa 78, 84, 88
Aphrodite 36
Aquarius 32, 34–35
Arcas 69
Archer, the 31
Ares 50
Argus 42
Aries 14–15
Artemis 28, 69
asterisms 6, 96
Astraea 24
astrology 6, 10–11, 105, 106
  see also zodiacs
astronomy 6, 10–11, 88–101, 105
Athena 23
Atlas 85
Australians, indigenous 49
Aztecs 11, 81, 94–95

B
Babylon 32, 36
  astronomy in 27, 50, 54, 77
  see also Mesopotamia
Big Dipper 69
Boar, Year of the 99, 100
Bull 16

C
calendars 10–11, 91, 96, 98
Callisto 53, 69
Cancer 20–21
Capricorn 32–33
Cassiopeia 76–77
Castor 19
Chakana 78
Children of the Sun 92
China 11, 27, 53, 73
  astronomy in 53, 73, 96–97
Chinese Zodiac 98, 101
Concordia 50
constellations 6, 96, 105
  see also stars
Crab, the 20, 21
Crux 78–79, 105

D
Dike 24
Dog, Year of the 99, 100
Dogon people 66
Dragon, Year of the 98, 100

E
Earth 46–47
eclipses 96
Endymion 49
Enki 32
Eos 28
Eros 36
Ethiopia 10, 77
Europa 16, 53

F
Fishes, the 36
Fish Hook 74–75
Four Stags, the 82, 83

G
Gaia 28, 46, 54, 57
galaxies 6
  Milky Way 64–65, 92
Ganymede 35, 53

Gemini 18–19
Goat, Year of the 99, 100
Gorgons 58
Great Bear, the 69
Great Crab, the 20, 21
Great Red Spot 53
Great Spirit, the 85
Greece, ancient 12, 39
  star myths 69, 77, 81, 85
  see also Solar System;
    Tropical Zodiac

H
Hades 61
Hawai'i 74, 88
Helios 41
Helle 15
Hera 20, 23, 42, 69
Hercules 20, 21, 23
Hermes 42
Hikoboshi 72–73
Hinduism 36
Horse, Year of the 98, 100
Hydra 20

I
Inca Empire 11, 46, 70, 92–93
India 11, 36
Inti 46
Io 42, 53
Italy 11

J
Japan 73, 84
Juno 42, 50
Jupiter 42, 50, 52, 53, 61
  and Saturn 54, 57
  see also Zeus

K
Kiowa people 85
Kronos 54
Krotos 31
Kukulkan 45, 91

L
Lakota people 85
Leda, Queen 19
Leo 22–23
Libra 25, 26–27

M
Māori 58, 84, 88
Mars 50–51
Matariki 84
Mato Tipila 85
Māui 74–75
Maya civilisation 11, 45, 90–91, 95
Mayu 92
Medusa 58
Mercury 42–43, 82
Mesopotamia 31, 36
  astronomy in 10, 28, 50, 69
  see also Babylon; Sumer
Milky Way, the 6, 64–65, 92
Minerva 58
Monkey, Year of the 99, 100
moons 53, 54, 57, 61
  Earth's Moon 48, 49, 96
Morning Star 45, 82
Mother Earth 46

N

Nemesis	27
Neptune	58–59, 61
Nereides	77
Nergal	31, 50
New Zealand (Aotearoa)	78, 84, 88
Nine Realms	82
Ninib	54
Norse mythology	82
North Americans, indigenous	85
North Star	96

O

Ops	54
Orihime	72–73
Orion	28, 81, 85
Orion's Belt	80–81
Ouranos	57
Ox, Year of the	98, 100

P

Pachamama	46, 94
Pacific Islands	10, 88–89
Pan	32
Pegasus	77
Persephone	61
Perseus	77
Phrixus	15
Pisces	32, 36–37
planets	42–61
planispheres	96
Plough, the	69
Pluto	60–61
Pollux	19
Polynesian peoples	74, 88
Poseidon	28, 58, 77
Proserpina	61

Q

Quechua people	70, 78

R

Rabbit, Year of the	98, 100
Ram, the	15
Rat, Year of the	98, 100
Rome, ancient	20, 39
see also **Solar System**	
Rooster, Year of the	99, 100

S

Sagittarius	30–31
San people	41, 49, 65, 81
Saturn	54–55, 57
Scorpio	28–29, 81
Selene	49
Seven Star-Sisters	84–85
Sirius	66–67
Snake, Year of the	98, 100
Solar System	7, 38, 39, 40–61
Southern Cross	78
stars	64–85, 86–87
see also **constellations**	
star signs (see **zodiacs**)	
Sumer	31, 50
see also **Mesopotamia**	
Sun, the	40–41, 92, 95, 96

T

Tahiti	88
Tanabata	73
Tangaroa	58
Taurus	16–17
Themis	25, 27
Tiger, Year of the	98, 100
Titan	85
Tropical Zodiac	12–13, 14–37, 106
Troy	35
Typhon	32, 36

U

Uranus	46, 54, 55, 56–57
Ursa Major	68–69

V

Venus	44–45, 50, 57, 82
see also **Kukulkan**	
Virgo	24–25, 27
Vishnu	36

W

wayfinders	78–79, 88
World Tree	82

X

Xhosa people	81

Y

Yacana	70–71
Yggdrasil	82

Z

Zeus	32, 35, 69, 85
family myths	16, 19, 23, 69
see also **Jupiter**	
zodiacs	7, 98–101, 106
Tropical Zodiac	12–13, 14–37

In writing this book, I have researched historical accounts, scientific findings and folktales from around the world. When it comes to myths, there is never just one version, and I have favoured tales of intrigue and inspiration. I hope that these pages will spark your own adventures in understanding.

Thank you to Amanda, Camilla and G, for cheering me on and accompanying me as this book came into being. — S.F.

To Mom for supporting my illustration dream and to Alison for encouraging me in all my projects. — C.P.

Astrologica © 2025 Quarto Publishing plc.
Text © 2025 Suki Ferguson.
Illustrations © 2025 Camelia Pham.

First published in 2025 by Wide Eyed Editions,
an imprint of The Quarto Group.
1 Triptych Place, London, SE1 9SH, United Kingdom.
T (0)20 7700 6700 F (0)20 7700 8066 www.Quarto.com
EEA Representation, WTS Tax d.o.o., Žanova ulica 3, 4000 Kranj, Slovenia.

The right of Camelia Pham to be identified as the illustrator and Suki Ferguson to be identified as the author of this work has been asserted by them in accordance with the Copyright, Designs and Patents Act, 1988 (United Kingdom).

All rights reserved.

No part of this publication may be reproduced, stored in a retrieval system, or transmitted, in any form, or by any means, electrical, mechanical, photocopying, recording or otherwise without the prior written permission of the publisher or a licence permitting restricted copying.

A catalogue record for this book is available from the British Library.

ISBN 978-0-71129-359-5

The illustrations are digital art
Set in Brandon Grotesque, Cherry Swash and Sagarana

Published by Debbie Foy
Designed by Lyli Feng and Magenta Fox
Commissioned by Hannah Dove
Edited by Hannah Dove and Katie Taylor
Index by Elizabeth Wise
Consultants: Claire Sipi and Lisa Davis
Production by Robin Boothroyd

Manufactured in Guangdong, China CC062025

9 8 7 6 5 4 3 2 1